The Perpetuation of Penitence

Benjamin Rodriguez

BookLeaf Publishing

India | USA | UK

Presentation by *BookLeaf Publishing*

Web: www.bookleafpub.com

E-mail: info@bookleafpub.com

ISBN: 9789360945923

First edition 2024

*To all those I've loved, to all those I will
love, but most importantly to all those who
have loved me and I was unable to love
them they way they needed.*

ACKNOWLEDGEMENT

Thank you humanity for giving us the ability to become anything we want to be. Whether it's suffering or happiness, it's an amazing thing to just be. All of this is to you.

PREFACE

Out with the old, in with the new, seasons of old come renewed. I promise this year better than last, let life, love, and loss go with the past.

For no matter how hard you try to withhold, how longingly you try not to be compelled, this life will leave you lost in its corrosive sands. So look at me now and grab a hold of my hand. I will carry you throughout all of eternity; your flesh, your despair, will all be a part of me.

But beyond the ethereal, the obscurity of it all, never stop looking forward, for I will always be there to catch you if you fall.

Never stop becoming better. The best support system starts with you finding the strength to help yourself. Be your number one fan.

La Luna

My luminescent, my sky, the apple of my eye.
An angel of the unknown, the lost, of oblivion.
Guiding ignorant souls through their sorrow,
wandering through their hallucinative dystonic
dominion.

Rising into the darkness, permeating through
your hardship, you shine beyond all measure,
dancing to your own courtship. Rising like a
spectacle of the ages, you invigorate all,
showering the skies with your love, life, and
call. Your love, the ambiance that engulfs me;
your comfort, the luster that cradles me.

Till your unexpected waning, your evanescence
slowly flickers away like a dying candle, and
consciousness becomes oblique.

Oh Eleadora, righteousness of the truest form,
far vast does humanity fall forever with their
axioms imbued, come save us now from our
asphyxiation and our rues.
Yet the sun's soft glow, the coming twilight,
forever reminding us of the unending prelude,
the biological rhythm, the earthly metronome,

time never stopping for this terminological
inexactitude.

Constantly you go, rising with the hopes and
dreams of many. Oh Lumina, what happens
when your trail is lost and you become bleary?

Thoughts man should not think, thoughts that
are intangible, yet is it possible to be in love
with the undefinable?

We shall see.

The Fallen King

Death to all who oppose us.

Split their skulls into fragments and mount them
upon your steed, their crowns.

Wipe the blood from your brow, and see through
red-strained eyes what lies before you.

Decadence, the paragon.

Decadence for all who shall choose.

The world for one man? No, one man for the
world.

The Untruths

You wish, you see.

Absence.

Void.

The Nightmare.

Hatred amongst the demon that lures.

Fighting, fading.

The Resurrection.

Epitome at its dying breath.

Phasing.

Surpassing.

The Wasteland.

Justice among the heartless sinners.

Carry me away, Far away into your arms, my sweet.

Fly me into the abyss, raiders scratching away as I go.

Tear me open, see what lies beneath.

Sometimes the truth is a lie, and sometimes the lie is the Domain.

Eat it.

Drink it.

Breathe it.

You wish... You shall see.

The Paradox

I am here because I have to be,
I am listening because you speak,
and I will stay because you call me.

I am dying because I'm near you,
I am contemplating when I'm away from you,
I am wishing because there has to be more,
I am understanding that nothing will amass.

I am subtle to think of my future,
I am weary to know what's best for me,
I am in pain when I grow away from you,

And I am leaving because that is what I need.

The Undiscerning Renitence

Through the maelstrom, there is serenity.

Through the calamity, there is happiness.

Through the anarchy, there is calm.

Love is a fickle thing.

I'd pick this little boat with you.

Sail with me.

The Glutton

Love is Beautiful
Find its Recourse
Claim its Throne
Chase its Everlasting.

Love is Pain
Embalm its Despair
Immolate its Congregation
Kneel to the Guillotine.

The only difference is who has the knife.

The soured reflection, a testament to the
insatiable ones.

The Promise

Time ceases for us.
Fate has acquiescence for us.
Our love trembles the universe.
Forever wanes for us.
Destiny is eclipsed by our fervor, for the gods
themselves are inconsequential to our courtship.

The stars and moon bore witness that night to a
love so pure that they could not help but stop
and stare.

The path is clear, so why do you falter? Till the
end of time I'll fight for you, but must you defer
to time's epilogue?

Find me, and I will be the brightest star in your
sky.

This I swear.

The Isles of Aspiration

Speak no more.

We've had our words.

Our final goodbyes.

Our time to talk has passed.

Our time to work things out has long passed.

Our time to say last words has come at last.

Sit at the table and see what's left.

Promises drenched in threats, if the flesh isn't portioned enough.

Ravenous hounds chomp away at the bits.

So take your share of me, after you've already torn me apart.

What little I have left, take a piece of that too.

There isn't happiness at the end of this. Only a different way to live.

Love is suffering for the benefit of another, and we've paid the toll many times over. Tears shed on both sides, enough to drown us both.

My love incapable, your love abridged. Regurgitation of confirmation. Reaction to inaction. Our pain supersedes the other's pain. "My tears fall far harder than yours ever could, my agony far greater!" Or so both sides claim. We give up an offering of pain but cannot offer remorse. The words are so simply said, but so meaningless now. Still, we say it to each other, the hollow husks of what we could've been. 'I love you,' still rings true, despite the connotation that now exists.

Silence. The remainder of zero. An empty room, nothing left but the ghosts of children running through the house. The finality. The death sentence. Silence. It is done.

We'll sit around and talk about what we could've been. The years more we could've had. We'll wake up from that soon enough, only to find the reflection is missing another. That day will never come, but let us dry out the eyes to prevent the coming tomorrow.

So let us dance in our dreams, the only safe place we have left. The world was never made for us, but in our dreams, anything is possible. In our dreams, nothing ever changed, and nothing was ever wrong. We made amends to our issues, we grew to water each other's garden. We made it. We have our happy ending. We finally made it.

And I loved you till the end of time.

The Delusion

Or so I tell myself every day as I watch you with your back turned to me...

You love me?
Yes, I feel it every day. The joy, its epitome, a fathom that is barely that. This horoscope, the kaleidoscope of my dreams. The clock that stayed frozen at 12 and 6, as I gazed into your longing eyes. Nothing can stop us babe.

Yes, you love me.
Yeah, sometimes it's not as smooth. But when is it ever? Relationships have their ups and downs, but we're meant to last. I've given you a blueprint of my love tank. You even have this book that you've been writing in every day because you're not an affectionate person. You don't like touching or kissing. You don't like words of endearment. You're perfect, though; you've said so yourself. Chaos is bliss when happiness is your world.

You love me?
You forget sometimes. Yeah, you stopped writing in the book, and in our notes. Yeah, you

said couples counseling was stupid. Yeah, you
said the homework she gave us was stupid.
Those were just not the routes for us, babe. I
know you love me; it cannot be any other way.

You do love me, sometimes.
I can't trust you sometimes. You say you'll do
something and you absolutely agree to it, then a
month later you revert back. No matter what it
is, how much pain I am in, you have never not
been one to stick to what you say. But I know
the days that you throw money into something,
those are the days you love me. Money can buy
love, right? I'm always your support, I'm always
there for you when you need me, but I
understand that you can't be there for me. That's
okay. I know my place, and I know you love me.

You do love me?
You can't hate me. Why do I think this? This
woman is everything I've always needed. She's
stressed at work. Angry at life. Yeah, she gets in
a rampage sometimes... all the time... but it's not
as often. Apparently for her own epiphany, but it
just so happened to coincide with our fallout?
I'm her rock. What's a little erosion for someone
you love? She'll reach the stratosphere because
I'll be the shoulders she can stand on.

I think you love me?
Your love, an infinitesimal idiom, colliding with
the universe like a thousand pieces of Scrabble.
Why is it hard to find? I don't remember it being
so hard to find... where is it?

...You don't love me?
This collage of imagery. I see us, happy. We
were always happy. You never hit me. You never
threw things at me. You never tried to. You had
good reasons. You never failed me. You did
everything I've always asked. I never had to
once ask you to love me. You've always loved
me. Why does this feel so surreal, though?
Things are so hazy sometimes.

...You don't love me...
You never did, not for a long time... why am I
crying? Why am I mourning as if I lost
something? I remember now. Somewhere
between the smiles and laughter was the agony.
Was me on my knees begging for your affection.
Almost 10 years, and you stopped loving me at
1. It's always the cold of night that comes with
the rush of reminisce. The warmth of hot air
permeating out of the vents. The music coolly
playing, with a reverberation bursting through
my chest. It's not the music, though. I remember

now. She doesn't love me. This pounding... it
hurts so much.

You promised you would love me. You promised
you'd stay. You promised you'd wait. You
promised there could never be another. You
promised to be what I needed. You promised that
you would make it up to me this time. You
promised that you'd change. You promised that
you'd take care of my heart. You promised so
many things, why? Why? Promises kept in
storage, never to be seen again. You never were
a keeper of the oath, words are just words after
all.

...but I love you...
Even when I know it's a lie. Even when I do
everything I can to make you happy. All you'll
ever see is that you didn't do anything wrong.
You're guilt-free because you can only be that.
You'll throw a bone in some ways, but like a
starving dog, I've learned that it comes with the
whip. So I sit there. Hungry. Suffering. Empty.
Living off the lies. Oh, how I can live off your
lies.

What am I doing? When did A turn to Z? I don't
know, but I know I don't want to be here
anymore.

100 on the dash, let's see what gives first. These tears halting, or my heart.

You'll always be perfect for me, my sweet. I know it's not true, but don't worry. I'll forget soon enough, and everything can go back to the way it was. You've always loved me in every way I could ever imagine. Everything will be perfect again...pain dissipates with time...ah...there she is. The girl of my dreams. The curation of perfection, that's what she always was to me. Let's build her up once more...let me forget once more...

Where were we again?

Oh yes, YOU LOVE ME!!!

Self-flagellation

Spite the tongue that drips acid weaved in stardust.

The frenulum of sanity and despair, find its focal point and exacerbate it until the blood clears from its veins.

Cut a little. Cut more. More. All of it. Cut it all.

Nothing's left? Cut my eyes out so I can't see how much I have done and how much is left I can go.

The Ouroboros

Far away in a time where there once was...

A home upon a hill, upon the well.
There was unwell on that hill which laid the
home.

Life blossomed between them, where they could
find themselves. They lost themselves, and all
was drained from their blossoms, its life.

An unlikely love fraught with the fear of the
unknown and the weariness, married with
strength and fortitude.

The gravity well weakening resolve, strength
sapped away, and fortitude begging to be given
up. Likely was their love to become weary once
more, for the unknown fear is all-consuming.

Bearing fruit, cultivating our forests, we thrived.

Poverty-stricken, our forests set ablaze by our
own hand, tossing our fruit by the call of the
fires, as if we forgot the blood and sweat that
was demanded.

Simple it was, our dream. Evoking the stories held deep in our hearts, we stride ever forward.

Forward in great strides sprinting into our demise, ripping out the pages of our hearts. A dream too simple to have body and soul.

It'll work out. Always has, always will. Dedication and perseverance, ever delaying the final act.

Skipping whole chapters to run amok. Rush to the end so that we can start the show once more. Let us show them how strong our dedication is, and how perverse we are. Let us show how it was, and what has been the race to decomposition.

For what is joy without an ending?

...The encore beckons.

Forever

Find me there.

Throw away the keys, for they are not needed when the locks have changed.

Discard the map, for it tells tales of a path long forgotten.

Pay no heed to the precepts of old, for the people no longer respect the forgotten traditions.

Fail to recall the tenets that ran the oligarchy, for they have been long usurped by drought and disease.

Burn the picture, for time has withered away the lines that once drew you to me.

Look past the energy, for the metamorphosis has changed the palette into colors that did not exist before.

Ignore the pheromones, for they no longer pair with the you history remembers.

So how do you find me?

Because a thousand lifetimes says you can.

The Despair of the Vain

Beknownst is the heart that finds its way through the dust cloud to find their diamond in the sky.

Shimmering through the nebulas of my soul, the etude, reverberating through states of consciousness, it takes from me everything.

Come think, woe is me. Come say, woe are they. Come now, let us sow woe to all that follow.

Drain me? Every ounce of life I'll partake. Reaper, come the acclaimed. Reaper, come the detained. Reaper, the lamented must be judged.

The light, unbearable. Infinite shadows dance upon their graves. Flashes of life blinking in and out of existence. Oh why they must be so muse? Why must they be so naive. Take from them everything. Take from them what they have taken from me. Watch as their wings flutter into ash as the incinerator eats.

Overwhelming. All-encompassing.

But how can I find you when I am everything?

The Sanctuary

Tears shackled to your face like an old room badly painted long ago. I fear myself to have hurt you, my love.

Yet I continue to watch as those crystalline structures fracture over time. Irrigated streams, years of erosion carving away into your flesh.

How I watch your face wither away. Dust to dust. I watch as you slowly burn away into specks of what used to be...as goes my love for you - which vanishes under the brilliant sparkle of the sun.

So I sit and bask in the ever-sinking sunset, reaching my hand out for you next to me. All that lies is a well-worn seat, and the dust slowly falling and refracting by not the sun, but by the rays of light you used to be for me.

I'll keep this spot warm for you. For now, I'll listen to the echoes of your melodies like a warm embrace, as if they are waves of the ocean upon the sands of my soul.

The Enigma

I can finally rest...let that darkness take over me.

Pulling out the knife and absolving the misery.

My tears fall for you, for I now know my place.

I'll see the pieces left and contemplate on trying
to patch them together. Maybe it's time to wake
up?

They're talking out of turn, falling out of style.
Where do I go from here?

I see the sun, though, in the distance slowly
ready to start the cycle.

Wipe my eyes, let me try again. This is worth it.

There you are. I finally found you.

If only it wasn't the other way around. So let me
lay my eyes to rest...because I finally lost you.

Woo Woo

Woo woo.

Whatchamacallit? That thin that be thinning. That wisp, that glorious wisp of your essence. That gravitas, that vulgarity, that raw. Tarrow that sits upon your empty throne. Their attendance empirical, for they do not know your influence.

Woo woo. It's giving a give that one can only give one way. Take the plunge because there's no way back. A tangent, the torment, twist me and break me. Put me back together with your spit and bile.

Woo woo, dadadadada. The piercing screech somehow muffled by the walls of defiance. How can I break through, how can I get you to love me too? Pass me the baton. Reach forward. Run...run...RUN!

You lie like a cheap rug. You tell me you're running. That you're jumping. You're not even looking in the same direction.

Up at night, I'll never be the same. All the
beautiful things, the nostalgia, it shatters me.
Every time we touch, it feels like you hate me. I
don't know why, but all around me I can see the
cigarette daydreams, that vanilla twilight. Where
that golden hour hits because you said you won't
let go. The sweet pillow talk we have had,
muddled by your mood. Well, maybe I am
stronger than you. I won't surrender, but I will
stop chasing after you. It'll be the last time that
you'll never see me again. So kiss me, because
I'd rather be someone to you. Dream girl, what
are we? Just give me a reason to give you all of
the stars.

I'll wait for you at the Bridge of Tomorrow.
Hurry, these doors are about to shut.

Casualty, the Causality of Casually

Another day, the divide between us. Greater still, does my love stretch thin for you. Our eyes meet. Disgust... disgust for myself and at you. Like a wart, you stain my life.

A stain I shan't live without. I stare at her from across the room, never has there been a luckier man than I. I see the twinkle in her eyes... your love radiates. The smile it brings me.

He smiles at me. His wretched smile. Melt his face off. If you ever tried you would've done more, been more, attempted more. Why must I get this version of you? This recycled piston breaking at any sign of turmoil. Freedom, the quandary of self-sustainment.

Quandaries, sustenance for the terror that quells. She's my rock, my soul, where would I be without her? Closer we sit, consuming each other's energy. Oh how much she fulfills me, trapped in her love.

Trapped. The annals of my predicament, I tread
in his domain ever pondering freedom.
Reluctance. Dissidence. Anarchy. To tear myself
from his flesh, like a suckling babe. Fear
controls me.

At times, fear comes about. How she can break
me in the simplest of ways. My heart is yours
forever, and I pray that you can keep it safe.

Safety, how it has long since abandoned me. To
break you like you break me. A thousand pieces
scattered in the wind and still it would be too
much of you in this world. The existence of you,
if I could erase it, the chains would be broken.

What is the purpose of my existence if not to
love you? A glisten in your eye. I cannot tell if
it's for me or for you. Oh how cute you are when
your love is so strong that you cannot hold it
together. Your grandeur absolute.

The cracks further worn, sanded down by his
unrelenting grandeur. Melt him down for scrap
as he has done to me. Who am I but useless
fodder for the masses. Use me, for that's all I
have to offer. A concubine and the rags on her
back. Use me till my dying breath.

Till my dying breath do us part. As if where I am right now is the center of the universe, our climax. Her love, the absolution that cleanses the sins of my past.

Absolution, the causality of stagnation. I have not the energy to bring me to task. Lacerations, by a thousand razors, unnoticeable to everyone but me. Slowly my blood percolates through his zone of adulteration, the perverse scythe coming to toe. Tear asunder the twin souls of this one. Upend my roots, with or without my consent.

Our tree, its roots deep in the soil. A soil so sound and pure, that even the strongest of droughts have no power. Steps away from the edge, to our forever.

The edge, I'm at the edge. I cry and plead, it falls on deaf ears. The dead whispering sweet sorrows, carving into me the images of a better resolution. Half-truths, but what is my life but a pile of lies. The delicatessen, layered deep, compounded into the globules of haves and dreams. My roars, a quasar into the future.

Her tears colliding with the roar of my love. Does she not hear? How can I fix what I don't know? I didn't do that. I changed. I am perfect

for you, don't you see? Let bygones be gone, for
the future awaits. Our seed needs us together to
grow.

Her Causality

I offer to you forgiveness, I offer to you
salvation.
Take from me my love, take from me my
trepidation.

A fair exchange, the limits.
A tell-tale, full of its gimmicks.

Romantic isn't it? The beauty of it all.
The exuberant rise, with the thundering fall.

The cardiovasculars, intriguingly small.
Come show me, the acute precision of a thrall.

Serrate through the bars, emancipation awaits.
Don't you dare falter, you must avoid your fate.

Draining, fainting, feel the attenuation.
Thinning, blackening, the mortal coil in
detonation.

Wings blossoming around me, its warmth
soothing me.
The sun's soft glow, the new day awakening me.

Peace...at...last...

His Casually

Peace...at...last...what do I do with that?
Endless thoughts of our future, razed by the
swing of the bat.

The grave sings her song, a song I could never
hear.
My heart bleeds for you, unable to translate that
I want to be near.

You didn't take me with you, not even a whisper.
It must've been enough, it must've been too
much for her.

I'm sorry for the pain, for the grief.
I'm sorry the attention to detail that was always
too brief.

Let me give you the only thing I have left.
I lay it out on the altar for you, the steel so deft.

Swiftly, I must run to her.
She still loves me, her love it lures.

Faster, deeper, paint the walls with my love.

Don't hesitate, she needs you, she waits for you
above.

Shred and mutilate it all.
I offer you every pound, ounce, till I fall.

My tongue, with forceps I tear the flesh
barbarically.
For why speak when my love falls empty
apically.

My nose, I bash it with the hammer.
For in her absence, her scent dissipates...nothing
matters.

My legs, I fillet them to the bone.
If only these legs ran in her direction, I would
not be alone.

My lips, I sear them to carbon.
Only in fire can my sins be pardoned.

My ears, I fill them with boiling oil.
Silence the world, its resonance a toil.

My eyes, I plunge my fingers to retrieve them.
A world without her, sight be condemned.

My hair...oh how she would run her fingers
through.
With this razor, I offer my scalp for you.

My hands, I am unable to do both.
Have my right, for it no longer has purpose
without your hand in oath.

All I have left is my body. I can barely move,
but you've always had all of me. You deserve it
all. Let the city write stories of our love, and the
lengths we'd go. Time to go.

Peace...at...last.

The Train

He waits for her, she leaves him to wait.
She waits for him, he doesn't wait for her.

He wipes his tears for her, she laughs at him.
She wipes her tears for him, he is stoic.

He needs time to process his future, for it looks
bleak.
She has no time to give. She lives on strides and
her own metronome, her future is now.

He knows that she's both good and bad for him,
but heartbreak reminds him of better times.
She knows he's good for her, but she thinks his
patience infinite.

He thinks she'd chase after him, but he knows
that putting hope in her has always failed.
She thinks time is subjective, the only time that
is of value is hers and now.

His pain, a hardship he'll hold for years. The
scars, stories to remember for years to come.

Her life, easy to fall back into place. His
presence, just a piece in her puzzle with a
thousand more exactly like it.

His life, stops time for her.
Her life, with speed bumps like him.

His thoughts, race for her.
Her thoughts, runs him through.

He knows he's not perfect, but he thinks he's
worth it.
She knows he's a man who doesn't deserve all
the truths.

So...when will he wake up? This dream, like this
train, is coming to the end of the line. Buy
another ticket and force this dream into reality?
Or awaken to face the reality that dreams are
meant to be out of reach.

I'll take both.

Serenity

Happiness is simple.

The ebb and flow of our spirits helixing towards Io. Their energies an equilibrium of osmosis. Their cations and anions, an endless fission of passion. Slowly though, the dark matter pulls away at them, inching towards the cavitation.

The Queen, a remnant of the King's shadow. Through darkness and light, she continues to be his strength. Her blood, the IV that straddles the world. Her body, the soapbox for him to become.

She fears his hand, for it is mighty and strong. Armies fall with every nock, as his aim is true. Appease the king, for he is gentle, but be wary of the hand for it strikes scorches the earth.

His anger, a premonition in the dark skies. Nail the coffin, without remorse. Turn away for his lightning strikes twice.

The Queen lost her way, trying to be the shade
and the sun for the King. How can one be
everything and still be nothing?

The King inches closer to the cliffside. The
rocks teeter as they gaze upon the helpless King.
The scythe, the pendulum arching towards his
demise. He wishes he had the time to make the
mistake and return, but the land is disappearing
all around him, and he has to move forward.

The King advances, the paradox that lies within.
Walk. Turn. Run. Stop. Turn. Jump. The
silhouette of Yggdrasil, tendrils entrenched into
the souls of the dead. Death fields lay barren
with the iron-soaked land. The cries come from
all sides. Where are you my Queen?

The same mistake that lies before him. Why has
he been here before? Whispers from the planes,
the ringing nostalgia, effervescently tinging his
eardrums. Everything changed, but her tears stay
the same.

Death is to ignore the cries of your lover. Life is
to kneel by her side.

What is required for forgiveness is built from the
erroneous.

Stagnation she calls. The muck trifled with lies
and regret.

Hasten. He moves forward with no regrets. A
home cannot be built on the shores of yesterday.
On the charred shoulders of the Queen, the King
shall stake his claim.

The path rocky, but from the veil, she murmurs
to be steadfast. The path will become firm and
full of life. By her will, does the land open up.

Fear, the complexities of love is that hate is at
the border. Timid is the heart without experience
of heartbreak. Scars and fissures line the rest of
us like shattered glass and hot glue. Balance the
Everclear by the blade of the flames or watch the
acids melt away the remains.

I will never forget you my Queen, for I am
everything because of you. The bodies doth lie
across the battlefield, but all I see is your
reflection in this deluge of blood. Your specter,
every morning, kills me. No matter how many
times I've killed you, you spit in my face.

I find a semblance of hope in the crumbs before
me. For surely, there must be a limit to how

much suffering the gods can entertain. The coming sun, my circadian rhythm, its hand forced to heel. Like a bud sprouting through stone, I can finally feel it.

Maybe in this life, maybe in this time, it won't be so bad. A place where even the butterflies can catch me.

Maybe.